T0087581

SWING WITH A BAND

Music Minus One

4229

SUGGESTIONS FOR USING THIS MMO EDITION

WE HAVE TRIED to create a product that will provide you an easy way to learn and perform these compositions with a full ensemble in the comfort of your own home. The following MMO features and techniques will help you maximize the effectiveness of the MMO practice and performance system:

Because it involves a fixed accompaniment performance, there is an inherent lack of flexibility in tempo. We have observed generally accepted tempi, and always in the originally intended key, but some may wish to perform at a different tempo, or to slow down or speed up the accompaniment for practice purposes; or to alter the piece to a more comfortable key. You can purchase from MMO specialized CD players & recorders which allow variable speed while maintaining proper pitch, and vice versa. This is an indispensable tool for the serious musician and you may wish to look into purchasing this useful piece of equipment for full enjoyment of all your MMO editions.

We want to provide you with the most useful practice and performance accompaniments possible. If you have any suggestions for improving the MMO system, please feel free to contact us. You can reach us by e-mail at *info@musicminusone.com*.

Music Minus One

4229

CONTENTS

©2009 MMO Music Group, Inc. All rights reserved.
ISBN 1-59615-805-0

Bb TENOR SAXOPHONE

DON'T BE THAT WAY

Benny Goodman, Mitchell Parish
and Edgar Sampson

DON'T BE THAT WAY
Benny Goodman, Mitchell Parish and Edgar Sampson
Copyright ©1938 by Robbins Music Corporation
Rights for the U.S. Extended Renewal Term Controlled by Ragbag Music Publishing Corporation (ASCAP),
Parmit Music and EMI Robbins Music Corporation
All Rights for Ragbag Music Publishing Corporation Administered by Jewel Music Publishing Co., Inc. (ASCAP)
International Copyright Secured   All Rights Reserved   Used by Permission

TENOR SOLO

TENOR SAXOPHONE

I'M THROUGH WITH LOVE

Gus Kahn, Matt Malneck
and Bud Livingston

I'M THROUGH WITH LOVE
Gus Kahn, Matt Malneck and Bud Livingston
© 1931 (Renewed) METRO-GOLDWYN-MAYER INC.
Rights for the Extended Renewal Term in the U.S.
Controlled by GILBERT KEYES MUSIC COMPANY and EMI ROBBINS CATALOG INC.
All Rights for GILBERT KEYES MUSIC COMPANY Administered by WB MUSIC CORP.
All Rights Reserved   Used by Permission of ALFRED PUBLISHING CO., INC.

MMO 4229

Bb TENOR SAXOPHONE

ROSE ROOM

Harry Williams and Art Hickman

TENOR SOLO - (MELODY)

ROSE ROOM
Harry Williams and Art Hickman
Copyright © 2009 Ramapo Music (BMI)
International Copyright Secured   All Rights Reserved
Used by Permission

MMO 4229

Bb TENOR SAXOPHONE

I'LL NEVER BE THE SAME

Gus Kahn, Matt Malneck
and Frank Signorelli

I'LL NEVER BE THE SAME
Gus Kahn, Matt Malneck and Frank Signorelli
© 1932 (Renewed 1960) EMI ROBBINS CATALOG INC.
All Rights Controlled by EMI ROBBINS CATALOG INC. (Publishing)
and ALFRED PUBLISHING CO., INC. (Print)
All Rights Reserved

MMO 4229

Bb TENOR SAXOPHONE

HOW AM I TO KNOW?

Dorthy Parker and Jack King

HOW AM I TO KNOW?
Dorthy Parker and Jack King
© 1929 (Renewed) EMI Robbins Catalog, Inc.
All Rights Controlled by EMI ROBBINS CATALOG, INC. (Publishing)
and ALFRED PUBLISHING CO., INC. (Print)
All Rights Reserved

B♭ TENOR SAXOPHONE

STOMPIN' AT THE SAVOY

Benny Goodman, Chick Webb
and Edgar Sampson

STOMPIN' AT THE SAVOY
Benny Goodman, Chick Webb and Edgar Sampson
Copyright ©1936 by EMI Robbins Catalog Inc.
Copyright Renewed by Rytvoc, Inc., Ragbag Music Publishing Corporation (ASCAP),
EMI Robbins Music Corporation and Razaf Music Co.
This arrangement Copyright ©2008 by Rytvoc, Inc.,
Ragbag Music Publishing Corporation (ASCAP), EMI Robbins Music Corporation and Razaf Music Co.
International Copyright Secured   All Rights Reserved   Used by Permission

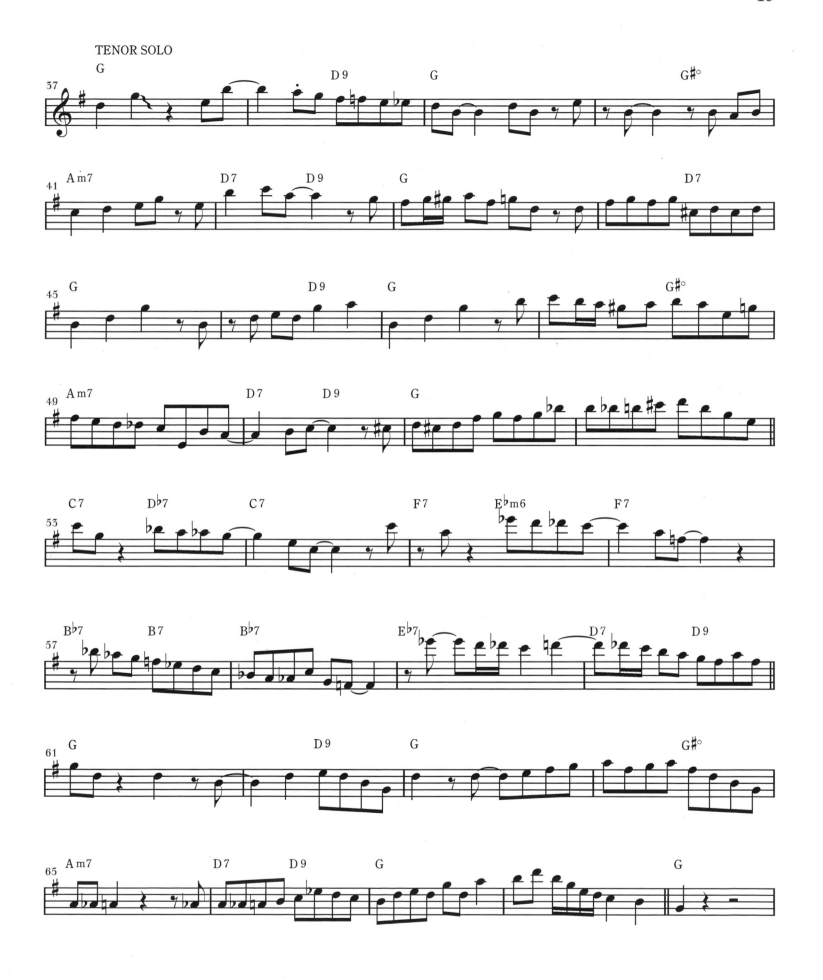

B♭ TENOR SAXOPHONE

I UNDERSTAND

Kim Gannon and Mabel Wayne

I UNDERSTAND
Kim Gannon and Mabel Wayne
© 1940 (Renewed) EMI WATERFORD MUSIC, INC. and EMI UNART CATALOG INC.
Exclusive Worldwide Print Rights Controlled and Administered by ALFRED PUBLISHING CO., INC.
All Rights Reserved

MMO 4229

Bb TENOR SAXOPHONE

WHAT CAN I SAY AFTER I SAY I'M SORRY?

Walter Donaldson
and Abe Lyman

WHAT CAN I SAY AFTER I SAY I'M SORRY?
Walter Donaldson and Abe Lyman
© 1926 MILLER MUSIC CORPORATION
Copyright Renewed and Assigned to EMI MILLER CATALOG INC. and DONALDSON PUBLISHING COMPANY
Exclusive Worldwide Print Rights for EMI MILLER CATALOG INC.
Controlled and Administered by ALFRED PUBLISHING CO., INC.
All Rights Reserved

MMO 4229

B♭ TENOR SAXOPHONE

I'M IN THE MOOD FOR LOVE

Jimmy McHugh
and Dorothy Fields

I'M IN THE MOOD FOR LOVE
Jimmy McHugh and Dorothy Fields
© 1935 (Renewed) EMI ROBBINS CATALOG INC.
All Rights Controlled by EMI ROBBINS CATALOG INC. (Publishing) and ALFRED PUBLISHING CO., INC. (Print)
All Rights Reserved

TENOR SAXOPHONE

I GOT IT BAD

(And That Ain't Good)

Paul Francis Webster
and Duke Ellington

I GOT IT BAD (And That Ain't Good)
Paul Francis Webster and Duke Ellington
Copyright © 1941 Sony/ATV Music Publishing LLC and Webster Music Co. in U.S.A. Copyright Renewed
This arrangement Copyright © 2008 Sony/ATV Music Publishing LLC and Webster Music Co. in the U.S.A.
All Rights on behalf of Sony/ATV Music Publishing LLC Administered by
Sony/ATV Music Publishing LLC, 8 Music Square West, Nashville, TN 37203
Rights for the world outside the U.S.A. Controlled by EMI Robbins Catalog Inc. (Publishing) and Alfred Publishing Co., Inc. (Print)
International Copyright Secured   All Rights Reserved

Bb TENOR SAXOPHONE

ONE O'CLOCK JUMP

Count Basie

ONE O'CLOCK JUMP
Count Basie
© 1938 (Renewed) EMI FEIST CATALOG INC.
All Rights Controlled by EMI FEIST CATALOG INC. (Publishing) and ALFRED PUBLISHING CO., INC. (Print)
All Rights Reserved

31

MUSIC MINUS ONE
50 Executive Boulevard
Elmsford, New York 10523-1325
800-669-7464 (U.S.)/914-592-1188 (International)

www.musicminusone.com
e-mail: info@musicminusone.com